Message from Gail Hillebrand

Associate Director for Consumer Education and Engagement

The mission of the Consumer Financial Protection Bureau is to make markets for consumer financial products and services work for consumers by making rules more effective, by consistently and fairly enforcing those rules, and by empowering consumers to take more control over their economic lives. Empowering consumers to take control of their financial lives and achieve their own life goals is a critical part of the Bureau's mission.

Consumers need four things to be financially empowered. First, consumers need consistent access and the ability to choose among high-quality financial services. Second, consumers need sufficient information about the costs, the benefits, and the risks, of choices in the marketplace. Third, consumers need a set of financial habits and skills that constitute financial capability to help them to make the financial decisions that benefit themselves and their families. Finally, consumers need to know that they can get a better shot at achieving their own life goals if they affirmatively seek information, make choices, and take steps to control their financial lives.

Consumers today are faced with increasingly complex financial decisions, many of which have long term consequences. When individuals don't have enough knowledge and confidence to navigate the financial marketplace, it may be harder for them to avoid financial problems. For many consumers it is essential to have a trusted resource for financial information, education and help navigating the many steps toward financial empowerment. This is especially true for people who are economically vulnerable.

The Office of Financial Empowerment is part of the Bureau's Division of Consumer Education and Engagement. It has a specific focus on low-income and economically vulnerable consumers. The work of the Office of Financial Empowerment is guided by the Dodd-Frank Act mandate to provide "information, guidance, and technical assistance regarding the offering and provision of consumer financial products or services to traditionally underserved consumers and communities."

The CFPB Office of Financial Empowerment recognizes that for some consumers, social service agencies serve as a trusted resource. Through our research and outreach, we have learned that case managers and frontline staff at social service agencies do not always have the knowledge, skills and tools to support their clients in improving their financial lives. As a result we took on the challenge of developing and testing a new set of tools and training for staff and volunteers working to help empower economically vulnerable consumers.

This report represents the results of our effort to learn what tools local service providers need to help their clients increase their financial capabilities. Through the field scan we contacted fourteen organizations that provide financial empowerment training to their case managers and frontline staff. We learned how programs have succeeded – or struggled – in providing training, tools, and resources to change case manager and client behavior. We conducted in-depth interviews of five organizations that represented diverse approaches to offering this type of training: Seattle-King County Asset Building Collaborative, United Way of Greater Cincinnati, Louisville Metro/Living Cities, The Financial Clinic, and the State of Minnesota.

The information and recommendations set forth in this report were invaluable in guiding the Bureau's work in creating a financial empowerment toolkit called *Your Money, Your Goals*. The toolkit is designed for training case management and frontline staff to help them gain the personal skills to be competent and comfortable in providing financial empowerment services to their clients.

In late 2013 we will be testing the effectiveness of *Your Money, Your Goals* with a diverse group of service providers. In 2014 we will share *Your Money Your Goals* broadly so that social service providers throughout the country can use this tool as they help their clients move toward greater financial stability and security. Our ultimate goal in this initiative is to bring reliable, unbiased information and practical tools within reach of millions of low income consumers so they can put it to work. As they use these tools, they will build the financial capability that equips them to make informed decisions that help them to take control of their financial lives and reach their goals.

Table of contents

Message from Gail Hillebrand 1

Executive summary 4

1. Introduction 8

2. Approach to the field scan 9

3. Definitions 11

4. Findings from the field scan 12

5. Transferability of the model to other locations 30

6. Conclusion 32

Appendix A: 33
 Summaries of in-depth interviews 33

Appendix B: 46
 Effective practice criteria 46

Appendix C: 48
 Case manager and financial education provider outcomes...........................48

Appendix D: 53
 Additional programs interviewed for scan..53

Executive summary

The Dodd-Frank Wall Street Reform and Consumer Protection Act of 2010 (Pub. L. 111-203) ("the Dodd-Frank Act" or "the Act") established the Consumer Financial Protection Bureau (CFPB) to regulate the offering and provision of consumer products or services under federal consumer finance laws. The Dodd-Frank Act establishes that a function of the Bureau includes "providing information, guidance, and technical assistance regarding the offering and provision of consumer financial products or services to traditionally underserved consumers and communities."[1] The Office of Financial Empowerment (Empowerment) within the CFPB is responsible for providing opportunities for low-income and economically vulnerable consumers to improve their financial capability.

Many economically vulnerable consumers benefit from connection to networks of public and nonprofit service providers to help address their immediate financial needs. For these consumers, frontline staff and case managers can be their link to programs, products and services that promote financial capability, such as financial education or coaching, safe and low-cost financial services, and free tax preparation services. What we have learned from the nonprofit provider community is that not all frontline staff have had the training and information they feel they need to offer financial empowerment services to their clients.

In 2012, CFPB identified and interviewed a small number of organizations that offer training programs to equip case managers with a basic understanding of the components of financial empowerment. These components include the role of asset-building in stabilizing economically vulnerable households, the importance of informed money-management decisions, and the availability of affordable financial services that meet their clients' needs. However promising

---

[1] 12 U.S.C. § 5493(b)(2)

this type of training, it was clear from discussions with practitioners in the field that it is not widely available in the majority of communities.

In fulfillment of the Bureau's statutory obligation, and informed by strong encouragement from the social service field and initial assessments of case managers who had completed similar trainings, the Office of Financial Empowerment developed a financial empowerment training toolkit, called *Your Money, Your Goals*, for social services programs. The Office also developed training materials to help local trainers facilitate workshops to increase case managers' understanding of financial empowerment principles and resources.

The first step in creating the CFPB's toolkit was to perform a broad scan of the field to identify effective existing training programs and to document best practices. To accomplish this task, Financial Empowerment engaged ICF International to conduct the scan and to document its findings.

This report summarizes the results of the national field scan, highlighting how programs that already train case managers have succeeded—or struggled—in their efforts to provide training, tools, and resources to change case manager and client behavior. The field scan, conducted from October through November 2012, included a high-level national inventory of organizations that are training case managers and other frontline staff in financial empowerment. The field-scan included in-depth interviews at five organizations whose work was of special interest: Seattle-King County Asset Building Collaborative (SKCABC), United Way of Greater Cincinnati, Louisville Metro/Living Cities, The Financial Clinic, and the State of Minnesota.

FINDINGS

The following findings represent themes that emerged from both the inventory and in-depth interviews of the field scan.

- **Finding 1:** *Case managers and financial educators have a common understanding of the financial issues and challenges facing clients notwithstanding differences in the context of service or geography.* The financial issues and challenges most commonly cited include: credit, debt, budgeting, income, banking or using financial services, and asset-building.

- **Finding 2:** *Case managers' level of motivation to learn financial empowerment varies widely.* Some case managers view their clients comprehensively and understand why, how, and where integration of financial empowerment may work; others may not. Also, some case managers have ongoing relationships with clients that provide many opportunities for integration of financial empowerment; others do not.

- **Finding 3:** *Case managers' lack of confidence regarding financial issues may be an obstacle to their integrating financial information into their work with clients, even following training.* Lack of confidence was widely cited by case managers as the primary reason the information provided in training was not used with clients.

- **Finding 4:** *Case managers struggle with when and how to incorporate financial empowerment into their work with clients.* The training provided to case managers and other frontline staff did not always answer one key question, which is: What do I do with this information now? Some programs responded by emphasizing referrals, while others created a tools-based approach.

- **Finding 5:** *Some programs encourage case managers to start the financial education discussion by learning first where the participant wants to start.* In some cases, this is determined through a simple assessment tool or a discussion about the client's goals. The assessment or information about goals provides a starting point for a discussion about their finances.

- **Finding 6:** *Because clients' financial issues vary broadly, some initiatives provide follow-up training, follow-up technical assistance, or a resource and referral network for case managers.* Organizations in the field scan used a variety of innovative strategies to address the need for ongoing support to case managers following financial empowerment training.

- **Finding 7:** *Even though the amount of training varied and many different curricula were used, the topics covered converged.* Some of these topics included setting goals, budgeting, saving for goals, getting free tax preparation assistance, avoiding the use of high-cost, debt-creating products or services, identity theft, frauds, and scams.

- **Finding 8:** *While some participatory training elements were incorporated into training, most were presentation-based.* Several programs incorporated core principles of adult learning, which include participatory exercises, to improve retention of material delivered in the training.

- **Finding 9:** *Most training initiatives targeted at case managers recommended some form of assessment of the effectiveness of the initiatives, but few tracked whether case managers* *were using this information with clients.* One program, the Financial Clinic, reported tracking this information once training had been provided to case managers or other frontline staff.

- **Finding 10**: *There were unanticipated benefits of training a large group of case managers and nonprofit staff in the same ways and using the same tools.* One example was creating a common awareness and understanding of the financial challenges facing clients; another was developing support systems for the case managers, because they recognized that they were all "speaking the same language."

- **Finding 11:** *Focused leadership and ongoing collaboration among partners can help to sustain and expand financial empowerment activities.* For many programs, institutionalizing financial empowerment has been an intensely collaborative process. Formalized collaboration with public, private, and nonprofit partners has been important for the continuation and growth of financial empowerment activities.

1. Introduction

The Consumer Financial Protection Bureau's (CFPB) Office of Financial Empowerment contracted with ICF International to develop a Financial Empowerment toolkit for social services organizations. The *Your Money, Your Goals* toolkit and training materials will provide a framework for training that supports the use of financial empowerment tools and techniques by case managers. This field scan report laid the groundwork for developing the toolkit by identifying how existing programs have succeeded—or struggled—in changing case manager and client behavior by providing training, tools, and resources. The report includes the following:

- Findings identified in a national inventory of programs that train case managers on financial empowerment, as well as in-depth interviews conducted with five organizations. The five participating organizations were Seattle-King County Asset Building Collaborative, United Way of Greater Cincinnati, Louisville Metro/Living Cities, The Financial Clinic, and the State of Minnesota,

- Narratives from the in-depth interviews (Appendix A),

- Effective-practice criteria (Appendix B),

- Case manager and financial education provider outcomes (Appendix C), and

- Additional programs interviewed for scan.

2. Approach to the field scan

ICF began the qualitative field scan with an inventory of programs of interest, which identified and described programs and initiatives providing financial empowerment services to case managers and other frontline staff. The contractor used knowledge of the financial empowerment field as well as unstructured interviews with key informants to identify fourteen distinct efforts to train staff serving clients in a variety of organizational, situational, and cultural contexts. It then conducted informal and open-ended conversations with many of these organizations to learn more about their financial empowerment approaches. The types of information collected included outcomes and strategies used, target audiences served, post-training expectations, and approaches to measuring results. The contractor provided an inventory of programs of interest which summarized the findings of its high-level review of programs in the field, recommended criteria for effective (best) practices, and recommended organizations to study in greater depth. Exhibit 1 lists the programs ultimately selected for in-depth investigation.

EXHIBIT 1: PROGRAMS SELECTED FOR IN-DEPTH INVESTIGATION

Program	
United Way of Greater Cincinnati	• Focus on providing financial education to case managers and other non profit staff • Working within the United Way context
Louisville Metro/Living Cities	• Working with people experiencing homelessness • Financial empowerment in a municipal context
Seattle/King County Asset Building Collaborative	• Providing training, referral resources, and opportunities for ongoing connections for anyone working with clients that have moderate or low income

State of Minnesota	▪ Financial-education coordination among state agencies, involving agency commissioners ▪ Financial education provided to hundreds of case managers and other nonprofit staff
The Financial Clinic	▪ Tools-based approach to financial empowerment ▪ Providing direct coaching services as well as capacity- building to case managers and other nonprofit staff

Other programs that gave input for this scan, in addition to the five programs that provided in-depth interviews, include United Way of Silicon Valley, United Way of King County (Seattle), Head Start Pilot Projects in both Pennsylvania and Massachusetts, Four Bands Community Fund (Eagle Butte, S.D.), The Rise Foundation (Memphis, Tenn.), Hopelink (Bellevue, Wash.), United Way of Greater Chattanooga (Tenn.), Cities for Financial Empowerment (National Office), and Local Initiatives Support Corporation (LISC) Financial Opportunity Center (See Appendix D).

The contractor conducted the in-depth interviews as free-flowing conversations, using a high-level discussion guide to keep conversations focused on topics of interest. To include a diversity of perspectives, the contractor interviewed a combination of financial-empowerment trainers, case managers, and other key individuals for each program. Notes from the interviews, as well as materials collected on each program or initiative, were summarized, analyzed, and organized into narrative profiles.

3. Definitions

Within the field, there are various terms used to describe the work of helping people learn about and use financial information in a way that helps them reach their goals and achieve financial stability. Common terms include financial empowerment, financial education, financial literacy, financial fitness, financial development, and financial capability. While organizations advocating one term over another may have a specific definition to differentiate their term of choice from others in common use, financial empowerment is used throughout this document except when discussing a specific program's work. In those instances, the respective organization's preference is used to describe the work that they do.

The people receiving service are also referred to in many different ways in the field: participant, saver, asset-developer, customer, and client are commonly used. Throughout this report, we use the term *client*, which is the term most commonly used by case managers.

Case managers in this report are individuals who work with clients. A case manager is anyone who assesses, plans, coordinates, monitors, and evaluates options and services to help a client achieve his/her health, human service, and economic needs. Case managers work in nonprofit, public and for-profit organizations. While case managers are the primary target audience, the term *frontline staff* is used because some staff who work with clients regularly are not called case managers (and they may not self-identify as case managers) even though they provide the same function.

4. Findings from the field scan

The following findings represent themes that emerged from both the inventory and in-depth interviews of the field scan.

Finding 1: Case managers and financial educators have a common understanding of the financial issues and challenges facing clients, notwithstanding differences in the context of service or geography.

Based on the field scan, as well as the in-depth interviews, the contractor learned that the clients of case managers and other frontline staff – primarily of nonprofit, community-based organizations – vary broadly in terms of programmatic contexts and types of interactions with clients. Often, they were described through the lens of the service provided, such as: individuals who are chronically homeless; survivors of domestic violence; meal center guests; refugees and immigrants; Head Start parents; individuals served by workforce development programs; individuals in transitional or public housing; and young people in foster care. All of the clients were moderate to low-income and had limited assets.

ICF also examined programs that serve urban areas, suburban and rural areas, an individual county, a multi-county region within a state, community members on an Indian reservation, an entire state, and various communities nationwide.

While the service context and the geographic location of the organizations reviewed throughout the field scan varied, there was clear commonality in the financial issues that financial educators, case managers, and other front-line staff felt the clients most often experienced.

Exhibit 2 summarizes those common financial issues and challenges reported by several organizations.[2] It should be noted that access to affordable housing was frequently cited by case managers as an issue that can be fundamental to long-term financial stability; however, training and solutions related to access to housing are beyond the scope of the CFPB financial empowerment training and as a result, are not included in this list.

EXHIBIT 2:   COMMON FINANCIAL ISSUES AND CHALLENGES

Financial topic	Issues and challenges
Credit	Having no or poor credit history, or having credit issues that prevent employment or access to financial and other services
Debt	Having too much debt, not understanding their debt situation (garnishments, collections, or other debt creating judgments), having medical debt in particular, or unsustainable levels of debt
Budgeting	Having too many expenses given level of income or not understanding their income and expense situation
Income	Not having income, enough income, or job opportunities
Banking or use of financial services	Using high-cost financial services because they are convenient or because clients are unbanked
Asset building	Having little to no understanding of assets, how assets help create a ladder out of poverty, and ways to build and protect assets sustainably

---

[2] This listing encompasses input from financial-education providers and case managers from Seattle King County Asset Building Coalition, City of Louisville Service Experts Team members, United Way of Greater Cincinnati, United Way of Silicon Valley, Rise Foundation, various practitioners from the State of Minnesota, and The Financial Clinic.

In most cases, an understanding of the client financial issues informed the financial-education content provided to the case managers, and the topics covered focused on the financial challenges clients most often face.

Finding 2: Case managers' level of motivation to learn financial empowerment varies widely

The motivation for acquiring financial empowerment skills varies widely among case managers. Some case managers view their clients comprehensively and understand why, how, and where integration of financial education may work for their clients. They tend to be self-motivated to learn and have less difficulty translating financial education to their work. This tends to hold true for case mangers already engaged in programs that have a financial component: transitional housing programs generally require clients to create a budget; transportation assistance programs require clients to budget as well as address credit issues; and financial education is an already-accepted practice for individual development account (IDA) programs. Finally, for some case managers, their organization or funder requires them to track financial outcomes. Financial empowerment training becomes a means to help them fulfill this requirement.

Other case managers have different perspectives when it comes to financial empowerment for their clients including:

- "It's not a part of my job."

- "The funders are requiring this."

- "I'm overwhelmed with my current job responsibilities and cannot hear this right now."

- "I only have a short time with clients (or only meet with them one time) and I have a lot to do in that short time."

- "I'm not doing a good job at managing my own finances. How can I help another?"

- "I'm willing, but I don't know how and I need to learn more."

There were generally three approaches used to get buy-in from case managers or nonprofit staff that did not have experience in financial education or did not work in a context that naturally included financial education concepts.

Approach 1: Involve organizational leadership.
Organizations that desired to offer financial empowerment training for case managers worked to increase buy-in from leadership of social services programs by:

- Hosting financial empowerment information sessions for chief executive officers and supervisory staff explaining the benefits of offering or integrating financial empowerment work within their agencies and through their case managers or frontline staff.[3] One organization even facilitated segments of the training for the CEOs and supervisors so they could experience the effectiveness of the training and the importance of the information.[4]

- Requiring the CEO's signature on an application from any case manager or nonprofit staff member wanting to participate in the training, in order to ensure that training participants will receive organizational support in integrating financial empowerment within their organization.[5]

- Charging for access to a financial development tool and requiring a contract that commits to payment for staff training and technical assistance."[6]

These organizations got buy-in from case managers and other frontline staff by using the organizational leadership and existing power structure within the agency.

Approach 2: Address case-manager concerns explicitly in the training.
Financial empowerment training begins with an invitation to case managers to share their concerns about implementing financial concepts and, in some cases, tracking financial outcomes

---

[3] Both United Way of Greater Cincinnati and RISE Foundation used this strategy.

[4] The Rise Foundation.

[5] United Way of Greater Cincinnati.

[6] The Financial Clinic.

with clients.[7] Then the training helps case managers understand financial empowerment outcomes and align their current program outcomes with those of financial empowerment. Case managers are shown how financial empowerment can help them help their clients more effectively.

Approach 3: Provide training only to those case managers that "get it."
United Way of Silicon Valley initially focuses its training efforts on staff members who already consider it important to incorporate financial empowerment into their work; it has not focused on engaging more reluctant staff. United Way hopes that as these staff members see their colleagues use financial education effectively in their own lives and with their respective clients, they will "come around."

Finally, case managers work in many situations: Some case managers see the same clients regularly (e.g., a vocational rehabilitation services case manager), while others may only have one opportunity to work with a client (e.g., staff at a meal center). Financial educators who have trained diverse groups of case managers recognize this and incorporate into their work examples of how case managers whose client contacts are of varying intensity and frequency can integrate financial education.

United Way of Greater Cincinnati reported that their original effort did not sufficiently help case managers translate financial education to their work context or provide them with guidance on how to "start the conversation" with clients across the spectrum. To manage this, they have begun segmenting case workers into three groups based on their levels of client contact:

- *Level 1: Short-term client contact.* This is generally a client addressing basic needs.

- *Level 2: Longer-term client contact.* This is generally a client in a program that provides some kind of transitional service such as a shelter or workforce development program.

- *Level 3: Extended/focused client contact.* This is generally a client involved in a long-term program such as an individual development account program.

---

[7] To varying degrees this is done by United Way of Greater Cincinnati, Seattle King County Asset Building Collaborative and The Financial Clinic.

Finding 3: Case managers' lack of confidence on financial issues may be an obstacle to their integrating financial information into their work with clients, even after training.

As one case manager described it, some case managers feel "they have no right to provide financial education information when their own financial situations are not in order." Case managers and other frontline staff who are asked to incorporate financial concepts into their work with clients may express the fear of not knowing enough, of telling someone the wrong thing, or instructing someone to do something they themselves are not practicing (the fear of being hypocritical). This was cited by all of the organizations interviewed as a core issue. Some sites structured their training to explicitly address this fear by using specific strategies to bolster case manager confidence while other sites discovered this through their work.

> 💬 **Promising Practice**
> The United Way of Silicon Valley trainees learn to use two tools by entering their personal information. This direct experience empowers them to more confidently pass information on to clients.

United Way of Silicon Valley, interviewed briefly during the field scan, developed its whole training program around two specific tools that the case managers and other nonprofit staff learn to use with their own financial information. To learn about how to get and read a credit report, they pull their own credit report through www.annualcreditreport.com and read it. To learn about credit scores, they order their educational credit scores generated by Credit Karma[8] (www.creditkarma.com). Through this process, they learn specific strategies to improve their own credit histories, remediate errors, and increase their own scores. By applying the information to their own situations, they feel empowered and better able to pass this information on to their clients. The program's creator/director explains it this way: "If you can understand your own situation more completely, you can help others."

The training that Local Initiatives Support Corporation (LISC) provides through the Financial Opportunity Centers and the training that The Financial Clinic offers to its client organizations

---

[8] United Way of Silicon Valley makes it clear that the Credit Karma Scores (TransRisk, VantageScore, and Auto Insurance Score) are educational only and that the scores used by lenders will likely be different.

through its toolkit also use a similar approach: Where possible, participants in the training use their own financial information to learn about and apply new financial concepts.

United Way of Greater Cincinnati instead facilitates discussions about how concepts taught in the training relate to or could help their staff address their own financial problems. This organization also explicitly covers values and attitudes about money as a way to improve case manager and nonprofit staff confidence and capacity to provide financial education. They also discovered that groups with experienced case managers and staff --such as those running individual development account (IDA) programs or from housing organizations -- did not struggle with confidence. On the other hand, those with little experience in asset-building or financial education generally were less confident about financial information.

> **Promising Practice**
> Recognizing that their clients may have different values, beliefs, and attitudes that result from their life experiences, the United Way of Greater Cincinnati provides experiential exercises to help case managers better understand people's differing beliefs and attitudes about money.

Their first session begins with an experiential exercise designed to help the training participants uncover and understand the experiences, individuals, and institutions that shaped their values, beliefs, and attitudes about money. This exercise helps case managers and nonprofit staff better understand the roots of some of their own financial practices that may be unproductive, while recognizing that their clients may have different values, beliefs, and attitudes about money resulting from their life experiences. This realization both increases case manager and nonprofit staff confidence and decreases the tendency to be judgmental about themselves or their clients.

Finding 4: Case managers struggle with when and how to incorporate financial empowerment into work with clients.

Training for case managers and staff does not always answer one key question: *What do I do with this information now?*

Financial education or financial empowerment services can either be presented as an additional service to be offered to clients, or integrated seamlessly into the workflow and client interactions of existing case management services. While integrating financial education does lessen common barriers experienced by stand-alone training or coaching programs— for example, promotion and recruitment of participants, transportation to sessions, or childcare—it requires significant planning by the organization and its staff. They must be able to figure out when to deliver what information to each client, which is more challenging than following a structured curriculum from session to session.

The United Way of Greater Cincinnati started the financial education training for case managers and nonprofit staff because so many organizations were trying to incorporate financial education as an "add- on" service. Those organizations were investing their time in marketing to and recruiting participants for financial education classes only to become repeatedly frustrated that their work did not result in reaching expected attendance levels, and to discover that they were actually spending very little time actually delivering financial information to clients.

While integration is the goal for United Way of Greater Cincinnati and many of the other initiatives profiled for this report,[9] case managers and frontline staff have not generally been given clear models for how, when and where to include financial information and education in the client transaction.[10] This lack of a practical model, combined with lack of case manager confidence could be part of the reason some case managers do not translate financial education training to their own work.

Finding 5: Some programs encourage case managers to start the financial education discussion by learning where the participant wants to start.

Programs that were able to initiate the "financial empowerment conversation" used multiple approaches. Some used money-related components of their program screening or processes as a launching pad for further conversation about money.[11] Others used discussion tools such as the following:

---

[9] Louisville Metro, The Financial Clinic, State of Minnesota

[10] The one potential exception to this is The Financial Clinic.

[11] Case managers in Minnesota that work in transitional housing, emergency rental assistance, or car loan programs utilized this technique.

- A **"life-satisfaction wheel,"** which asks participants to rank from one to ten their satisfaction with eight different areas of their lives. "Finance" is one of the eight areas, and a ranking less than ten generally opens the door for a discussion about finances with the client.[12] Also, financial issues often come up as clients describe their issues in the other seven life areas: personal/spiritual development, physical environment (home and workplace-based), career or business, family and friends (community), romance/intimacy, health/self-care, and social/fun.[13]

- A **list of resources** that are of potential interest to clients. Clients choose from the list those which most interest them. Many of the resources have a financial component, which allows the case manager to initiate the financial empowerment discussion.[14]

- The **Family Service Plan for Head Start.** This has several goals, including financial, toward which a family can work. When a Head Start parent lists the financial goal at the beginning of the program year, the Family Services Specialist asks parents where they want to start.[15]

Other financial education initiatives favor a simple assessment tool to find out about a client's goals or where a client may be struggling. The assessment provides a starting point for a discussion around finances.

Finding 6: Because clients' financial issues vary broadly, some initiatives provide follow-up training, follow-up technical assistance, or a resource and referral network for case managers.

---

[12] This tool is used by Head Start Family Specialists in Minnesota and Massachusetts, as well as by LISC.

[13] Laura Whitworth et al., *Co-Active Coaching* (1998)

[14] State of Minnesota

[15] Head Start in Massachusetts

While training can provide case managers with knowledge and tools that may increase their confidence in using this information with clients, issues may arise with clients that are beyond the capacity of the individual case manager.

Sites have managed this in several distinct ways:

- Provide a "**hotline**" that case managers can call to have their specific questions answered during set hours.[16]

- Provide an "**ask a counselor**" service on a website through which case managers can request information or ask specific questions. The questions, which are sent to state cooperative extension staff, are answered within forty-eight hours.[17]

- Provide **follow-up technical assistance** through contractual arrangements.[18]

- Provide opportunities for case managers and other front line staff to **join a peer network** and enroll in post-training workshops to continue the educational process.[19] The Seattle King County Asset Building Collaborative also has special-topic work groups, which study particular issues in depth. Currently, case managers and other frontline staff can join a Disability Initiative work group, a Medical Debt work group, and a Providing Services to Veterans work group.

- Provide a **handbook** that includes resources and referrals by topic. SKCABC modified *Your Money Helpline* created by the New York City Office of Financial Empowerment to make it specific to King County, Washington, while United Way of Greater Chattanooga

---

[16] United Way of Silicon Valley

[17] State of Minnesota on the *Help Minnesota Save* website.

[18] The Financial Clinic.

[19] Seattle King County Asset Building Coalition, the State of Minnesota, The RISE Foundation, and The Financial Clinic.

developed a financial education resource guide to support staff answering 2-1-1 calls.[20] Staff members of 2-1-1 are trained to screen callers for potential financial issues and then refer them to the appropriate organization for additional or ongoing financial education, counseling, or coaching assistance.

- Provide a **web-based portal** where case managers and other nonprofit or frontline staff can access information and tools to increase their own capacity or to use with clients. Developing a web-based toolkit was part of the United Way of Greater Cincinnati's original concept of providing training that is supplemented with ongoing access to online resources and tools. The State of Minnesota also has a website dedicated to providing resources for both clients and case managers.

- Provide clear **links to referral sources** as a part of the training process. Two sites in particular, SKCABC and United Way of Greater Cincinnati, have developed their empowerment training for case managers to refer clients for expert assistance with financial issues appropriately.

In the United Way of Greater Cincinnati case worker training, each of the four sessions includes information and exercises related to the topics outlined for the first half of the training. The second half of the training includes representatives from potential referral organizations who talk about the content covered as well as the services their organizations offer and when to refer a client to them. For example, the budgeting session includes traditional information and tools on budgeting and is then followed by presentations from programs whose mission includes providing financial education; representatives from Bank-On Cincinnati; and representatives from Cincinnati Saves. This process was repeated for the sessions on financial services, credit and identity theft, scams, and frauds.

- SKCABC holds one-day training sessions and includes a wide range of referral partners as part of the training; the partners participate in the training and provide presentations throughout the day linking their services to the content.

---

[20] 2-1-1 is a call-in clearinghouse commonly staffed 24 hours per day to connect people in need with food, housing, employment, health care, counseling, and other resources. These are often operated by United Way agencies on a city, county, or regional basis.

Finding 7: Even though the amount of training varied and many different curricula were used, the topics covered converged.

Exhibit 3 (page 26) summarizes the length of the training provided by some of the organizations, as well as the curriculum they used to train case workers or other frontline staff. The training ranged from four hours to thirty hours. There was little overlap in the curricula used except *Money in Motion*, which is used by two of the sites. Even with these differences in curricula, many of the topics covered were common:

- Setting goals

- Budgeting

- Saving for goals

- Automating savings; saving regularly

- Getting and reviewing credit reports; correcting inaccurate information

- Understanding credit scoring

- Using strategies for reducing or eliminating debt

- Filing for tax credits and planning the use of tax refunds

- Getting free tax preparation assistance from IRS-trained volunteers at VITA sites

- Using financial services (banks and credit unions) and managing checking accounts

- Avoiding the use of high cost, debt-creating products, or services

- Knowing where to get more help for debt management, credit building, budgeting, paying bills, and using financial products and services

- Identity theft, frauds, and scams.

There were a number of topics covered by only one or two organizations. These included:

- Keeping track of bills; setting up systems for paying bills on time

- Conducting debt validation

- Managing cash flow

- Saving for emergencies or unplanned expenses

- Psychology of money; values, attitudes, and beliefs about money

- Critical thinking

- Behavioral economics

- Vehicle and home purchase

- Career and education planning

- Risk management and insurance

- Investing basics and retirement planning

- Estate planning

EXHIBIT 3: LENGTH OF TRAINING AND CURRICULA USED

Organization	Training length	Curricula Used in Training Case Managers or Other Frontline Staff
Seattle King County Asset Building Collaborative	1 day, from 9:30 a.m. to 3:30 p.m. (4 hours of contact)	The Seattle King County Asset Building Collaborative developed its own training using other resources. The training is delivered via PowerPoint presentation.
The State of Minnesota	4 two- to three-hour sessions (8 -12 hours of contact)	The State of Minnesota uses *Four Cornerstones of Financial Literacy*, a curriculum developed by a credit counselor in Minnesota and used by most practitioners in the state. (Over 1,400 case managers, nonprofit and other staff have been trained through *Four Cornerstones*.)
United Way of Greater Cincinnati	4 half-day trainings (16 hours of contact)	United Way of Greater Cincinnati uses the *FDIC Money Smart* curriculum, modified it with some additional activities, and then added time with referral partners in each session.
Louisville Metro/Living Cities	5 two-hour trainings (10 hours of contact)	Louisville Metro/Living Cities contracts with Apprisen to provide its training using *Money in Motion*.
The Financial Clinic	2.5 to 3 days of training (depends on organizational contract); (15 to 18 hours of contact)	The Financial Clinic developed its own toolkit based on a scan of existing financial education materials.

Four Bands Community Fund (Eagle Butte, South Dakota)	3 four-hour sessions (12 hours of contact)	Four Bands uses three curricula in its training: *Credit Where Credit is Due*, *Money in Motion* and *Making Waves*, its own curriculum.
RISE Foundation	3 two-hour sessions (6 hours of contact)	RISE developed its own curriculum called *Common Cents*.
LISC in Financial Opportunity Center Communities	5 days (up to 30 hours of contact)	LISC contracts with Central New Mexico Community College to provide its Financial Coaching Training.

Finding 8: While some participatory training elements were incorporated into training, most were presentation-based.

The materials and the information gleaned from the in-depth interviews indicated that some participatory techniques are included within most training sessions. This is an important feature as it reflects the core principles of adult learning; it is likely to improve retention of material delivered in the training. The trainings appear to be presentation-led and include some application of information within the training context. This is especially true for those programs that take a tools-based approach to the training or have the case managers and other training participants learn through applying concepts to their own personal situations.

Other approaches used include facilitated discussion, case studies and some role-playing, as well as guest speakers. (Guest speakers are used by the two sites that invite referral partners, SKCABC and United Way of Greater Cincinnati.).

Finding 9: Most training initiatives targeted at case managers recommended some sort of assessment of the effectiveness of the initiatives, but few tracked whether case managers were using this information with clients.

It was difficult to ascertain through the interview process the extent to which programs were actually implementing their evaluation plans. Of all the programs reviewed or for which interviews were conducted, only two were able to provide actual evaluation reports: FAIM in Minnesota and United Way of Greater Cincinnati. The FAIM evaluation focused on financial literacy in the context of an IDA program. The United Way of Greater Cincinnati's evaluation examined the following outcomes among the case managers and nonprofit staff that had attended its training program:

- Improved financial education resources

- Increased staff knowledge of resources

- Improved agency capacity to provide financial education services

- Ability to better serve clients

- Overall satisfaction with training

Those who participated in the project ranked themselves using Likert scales[21] or by answering *yes* or *no* to the following statements:

- The training received by our staff through this pilot project was valuable to our agency.

- Participation in this project improved the quality of financial education resources our agency is able to offer to our clients.

---

[21] A Likert Scale typically measures strength or intensity of opinion or preference (An example is a five point scale such as strongly agree, agree, no opinion, disagree, strongly disagree)

- As a result of this project our staff knows where to obtain quality financial education teaching materials.

- We were able to improve our program and services because of the training and resources received through this pilot project.

- Participating in this project increased our agency's internal capacity to provide financial education to our clients.

- Would your agency consider utilizing an outside resource (such as community banker, etc.) to provide financial education to your clients?

Neither the State of Minnesota nor United Way of Greater Cincinnati were measuring whether case managers and other nonprofit staff were using the information once trained. Only The Financial Clinic reported tracking this information once training had been provided to case managers or other frontline staff.

Finding 10: There were unanticipated benefits of training a large group of case managers and nonprofit staff in the same ways and using the same tools.

At three sites in particular – the State of Minnesota, Louisville Metro/Living Cities, and the greater Chattanooga area – large numbers of individuals were trained using the same financial education or empowerment curriculum and the same tools. Four identified benefits resulted from this approach and the potential exists for additional systemic benefits in the future.

- There was a common awareness and understanding of the financial challenges facing clients of case managers and other frontline staff, and a common understanding of how to address some of these problems using the financial information, tools, and referral resources provided in the training.

- Clients with low incomes, including clients who were homeless, were given information effectively with "one voice" as they accessed different services or "shopped around" for financial and other consumer services.

- A common approach created a community support system for the case managers, because they were all "speaking the same language" when discussing financial concepts and financial empowerment outcomes for their clients.

- When communities develop a common practice of providing financial education to case workers and front line staff, it may be easier to make the case to state agency leaders and government officials. This bottom-up approach can promote collaboration among community stakeholders, government officials and policymakers, as demonstrated in Minnesota where ten state commissioners are working together to integrate financial empowerment throughout their respective agencies.

Increasing market-penetration with financial education content and tools could create systemic change and a greater overall awareness of the significance of financial empowerment to many aspects of community members' lives, irrespective of income levels.

This approach also has the potential to provide a solid foundation for assessment and evaluation: If all providers are working toward the same general financial empowerment outcomes, assessment and evaluation efforts can be more easily aggregated to demonstrate impact among a variety of target populations and segments, much as the IDA field did a decade ago.

Finding 11: Focused leadership and ongoing collaboration among partners can help sustain and expand financial empowerment activities.

For many programs studied as part of the field scan, institutionalizing financial empowerment has been an intensely collaborative process. Formalized collaboration among partner organizations and agencies has been important for the continuation and growth of financial empowerment activities. For example, Louisville Metro's Department of Community Development coordinates a working group of case workers from thirteen homeless services and housing agencies along with municipal and nonprofit leaders. This has led to common assessment tools, common financial empowerment activities, and common measures. Minnesota's governor and the commissioners of ten of its state agencies are conducting a scan of current financial education efforts and promoting sustained efforts to increase the financial capability of the state's residents.

5. Transferability of the model to other locations

All of the programs examined as part of the field scan were reviewed for transferability. The purpose was to assess:

- Whether the approach can be used in another geographic location

- Whether it can be used with a different target audience

- Whether the same kind of outcomes can be expected if the geographic location and clients are different.

Based on the review of all of the models, there are five promising approaches that are highly replicable.

- **Train all case managers and nonprofit staff using the same financial empowerment curriculum.** As noted in the *Findings* section, this provides a common base of knowledge among the case managers and nonprofit staff. This commonality facilitates networking among the individuals trained. A common curriculum also provides a foundation for common assessment (changes in knowledge, attitudes, behaviors, skills, and economic condition) and evaluation. This was most clearly demonstrated by the state of Minnesota (which used *Four Cornerstones of Financial Literacy)* and Louisville Metro/Living Cities.

- **Use a tools-based financial empowerment curriculum.** Using tools, instead of simply disseminating information, is important because it helps case managers and clients translate knowledge and concepts to their own lives. This approach was used by The Financial Clinic and United Way of Silicon Valley.

- **Build flexibility into case managers' use of financial empowerment information and tools with clients**. This enables case managers and frontline staff to match content to a client's goal or most pressing financial issue and then present other content or tools as they are needed. This approach was most clearly used by The Financial Clinic.

- **Focus the training on helping case managers address their own financial issues.** Most of the organizations interviewed recognized this was central to gaining case manager buy-in, as well as increasing their personal financial competence and confidence. United Way of Silicon Valley, LISC, and The Financial Clinic strongly emphasized using participants' personal financial information in the context of training. The State of Minnesota, United Way of Greater Cincinnati, and SKCABC recognized this was important, and they facilitated discussions and other activities relating to personal financial issues in the context of the training. While this approach is transferable, access to personal information may be limited in some communities because of the direct costs associated with acquiring it (e.g. FICO scores) or because there is limited access to technology.

- **Ensure the materials work with culturally diverse audiences as well as those with limited literacy levels.** Several of the organizations studied worked to ensure materials were culturally relevant across age, ethnic, urban/rural, and other characteristics of participants. However, fewer focused on the need for ensuring materials are literacy-level appropriate. Both aspects are central to making the content accessible for clients and the model transferable. SKCABC most clearly articulated this aspect of the model.

6. Conclusion

The findings and best practices identified through this scan, along with additional input from participants, expanded the breadth and depth of background information that has helped shape the design and development of CFPB's *Your Money, Your Goals: A Financial Empowerment Toolkit for Social Services Programs*. The CFPB is currently field-testing the toolkit to determine its effectiveness in enhancing the financial empowerment capabilities of case managers and frontline staff. This process will help ensure that its information and tools become a practical and valuable resource for social services staff and the low-income consumers they serve.

APPENDIX A:

Summaries of in-depth interviews

The Financial Clinic

SITE OVERVIEW

The Financial Clinic is a nonprofit organization based in New York City which focuses on helping low-income individuals and their families "build financial security" through specific financial development services. [22] It serves clients directly and through partnerships with other organizations in the greater New York City area. It also provides business-to-business capacity building services to public sector, nonprofit, and for-profit organizations throughout the U.S.

FINANCIAL EMPOWERMENT WORK

The Financial Clinic provides on-site financial coaching at Single Stop Sites, Financial Empowerment Centers, and community tax sites throughout the five boroughs of New York City and New Jersey. It has created a toolkit that covers five topic areas:

- Assets – emphasize consistent savings and increasing income by getting employer-based and public benefits.

- Banking – helps clients access low-cost financial services.

---

[22] The Financial Clinic used the term "financial development" instead of "financial education," "financial capability," or "financial empowerment."

- Credit – focuses on building a positive credit history and improving credit scores by remediating errors or negative information on credit reports.

- Debt – helps clients reduce their debt by developing actionable plans and advocating to creditors on behalf of their clients.

- Taxes – helps clients plan for and file taxes and productively use their tax refunds including tax credits for which they may be eligible.

This five-topic framework is also used with clients in the financial coaching process and forms the basis for the training provided to case managers and other frontline staff.

The Financial Clinic uses financial coaching, a relationship designed to last between three months and a year, to help ensure clients are supported in their own decision-making through focused processes that include examinations of their own finances. The Toolkit provides specific protocols for coaches to use with clients as they address assets, banking, credit, debt and taxes with each client to achieve the client's goals and financial security.

The Financial Clinic has a proprietary and detailed outcomes-based tracking system they have retooled and are making available to other organizations through a fee-based membership structure. Called "The Change Machine," this online system tracks over eighty measures related to financial development. Among the measures tracked are consistent savings (measured by three successive automatic deposits), changes in credit scores, changes in debt levels, and whether of a portion of the tax refund is used by a client to reach his/her financial goals.

KEY FINDINGS WITH MODEL

Discussions with staff and review of materials affirmed the importance of three specific concepts:

- Use of an outcomes-based framework, which facilitates content focus and provides a foundation for assessment and evaluation.

- Use of a tools-based approach for the development, organization, and delivery of the content, which allows those being trained to translate information to actions.

- That financial empowerment must take place in a "judgment-free zone."

Unlike other programs, The Financial Clinic does not emphasize referrals or resources beyond its toolkit, which specifically focuses on the five core topic areas defined by the organization as the five pillars of financial security: assets, banking, credit, debt, and taxes. The Financial Clinic also strategically works with networks that have a broader reach than any single agency. For example, in partnership with United Way of New York and the Human Resources Administration, The Financial Clinic developed customized tools and training for case managers and other frontline staff members in the domestic violence shelter system to help them understand how financial empowerment works to support an individual's ability to build confidence, regain control, and establish financial security.

Through their toolkit, which is disseminated outside of the greater New York City area via business-to-business contracts, they provide a standardized training and robust set of measures that focus on use of financial knowledge.

Finally, The Financial Clinic maps the connection of financial knowledge with financial actions and transactions in a step-by-step approach outlined in their toolkit.

United Way of Greater Cincinnati

SITE OVERVIEW

United Way of Greater Cincinnati provides services to a ten-county, three-state region, which includes communities in southwestern Ohio, southeastern Indiana, and northern Kentucky. This organization focuses its work in three core areas:

- Education – ensuring children are prepared for kindergarten and that youth succeed in school and life.

- Health – ensuring people have access to ways to improve their health and enhance their independence.

- Income – helping families achieve financial stability.

United Way of Greater Cincinnati seeks to bring about these changes by engaging directly in "community impact" work, raising money to support other organizations working to bring about results in its three areas of focus.

FINANCIAL EMPOWERMENT WORK

The United Way of Greater Cincinnati provides financial education training for case managers of community-based organizations that offer employment, housing, financial education, workforce training, child care, and emergency (food and shelter) services throughout the Greater Cincinnati area. The goal is to increase case managers' comfort with financial management tools and terms enabling them to deliver financial information more easily to the people they serve. United Way of Greater Cincinnati provides case managers and other nonprofit staff members with:

- A four-session, 12-hour training using the FDIC *Money Smart* curriculum augmented with "psychology of money" exercises and content, as well as information about identity theft, fraud, and scams.

- An introduction to local financial empowerment resources so case managers and other frontline staff members are able to refer their clients for additional or more in-depth financial management assistance appropriately.

- An online toolkit, developed in partnership with the University of Cincinnati Economic Center, for case managers and other frontline staff members to access following the training.

United Way of Greater Cincinnati expects that case managers and other frontline staff receiving the training will:

- Increase their knowledge of financial concepts (budgeting, savings, and credit repair).

- Feel more confident in their ability to make financial decisions.

- Increase their knowledge of how to improve credit rating/scores.

- Establish financial budgets.

- Maintain a budget (pay bills on time).

- Increase their confidence in sharing financial education and resources with clients.

IMPORTANT FINDINGS WITH MODEL

A review of their materials and an interview with United Way of Greater Cincinnati staff identified the following key findings related to this model:

- To help ensure case manager and frontline staff buy-in, United Way of Greater Cincinnati hosts information sessions for organizations' CEOs and supervisors. To ensure that organizations are committed to integrating financial empowerment into their existing work, they also require CEO signatures on applications for staff who participate in the financial education training.

- After doing an assessment, they discovered that vast differences in skills, motivations, and knowledge that nonprofit staff and case managers bring to financial education work. They then decided to focus on both knowledge and local resources and redesigned the training to provide financial education content and tools along with an introduction to referral resources related to the topics covered in the session. This formula was used in each session. For example, the budgeting session now includes information and tools on budgeting plus presentations from financial education programs, representatives from Bank On Cincinnati, and representatives from Cincinnati Saves. This was also done for the sessions that focused on financial services, credit, identity theft, financial scams, and fraud.

- After conducting the first round of training, United Way of Greater Cincinnati added activities and content that address values and attitudes about money as a way to improve case manager and nonprofit staff confidence and capacity to provide financial education. This exercise helps case managers and nonprofit staff better understand the root causes of some of their own financial practices and to understand that their clients may have different values, beliefs, and attitudes about money as a result of their life experiences. These activities increase case manager and nonprofit staff confidence, and decrease the tendency to be "judgmental" about themselves or their clients in terms of financial behaviors and practices.

- They also discovered that groups with experienced case managers and staff (individuals running IDA programs or from housing organizations) did not struggle with confidence. Those with little experience in asset building or financial education generally lacked confidence about financial matters.

United Way of Greater Cincinnati partnered with the University of Cincinnati Economics Center to design, administer, and analyze pre- and post-training competence. They have not yet tracked whether case managers are actually using the information and tools provided in the training with their clients, but plan to conduct follow-up surveys to learn more about confidence and use of financial information and tools by case managers and other nonprofit staff members.

In considering its program, United Way of Greater Cincinnati staff felt that the training did not do enough to help case managers translate financial information and tools to their respective work contexts or provide case managers with enough guidance on how to "start the financial conversation" with clients. This is something they plan to address in future trainings.

Seattle-King County Asset-Building Collaborative

SITE OVERVIEW

The Seattle-King County Asset-Building Collaborative (SKCABC) is a coalition of over 80 public, private and nonprofit organizations based in Seattle, Washington, and serving all of King County.

SKCABC focuses on connecting the organizations within the collaborative to build a "system of high-quality, accessible financial empowerment services and interconnected networks to deliver these services throughout King County." The Collaborative focuses on providing access to affordable, mainstream banking; financial planning, education, and coaching; credit and debt counseling; free tax preparation; access to public benefits; microenterprise development; and homeownership and foreclosure prevention resources.

FINANCIAL EMPOWERMENT WORK

In addition to referring individuals and organizations to financial education providers throughout King County, SKCABC provides training directly to anyone working with individuals and households that have low- to moderate-income. This is a broad audience, but includes primarily case managers and staff from a wide range of nonprofit service providers, as well as individuals from workforce development programs, the City of Seattle, and increasingly, medical professionals (e.g., mental health case managers).

The training is four hours long and covers:

- An introduction to SKCABC

- Introduction and rationale for the "learn, earn, save/invest, and protect" framework

- How to refer clients to services within the collaborative network

- Concentrated information on credit and debt issues

SKCABC uses small-group work, case studies, presentations, a question and answer session with credit counseling agencies, and storytelling during the training to convey financial empowerment information to the case managers and other nonprofit staff. The goals of the financial empowerment training are to increase case manager buy-in that financial empowerment and asset building are important, to help them start related conversations with their clients, and to encourage them to refer their clients to community-based resources. Representatives from resource and referral organizations participate and make presentations to encourage case managers to make referrals. The training is not designed to ensure case managers can solve clients' financial problems, but to help case managers have the right tools, information, and resources to give the clients a "nudge in the right direction."

Finally, all training participants are provided with a copy of *Your Money Helpline*, a topically-organized referral guide based on a tool designed by the New York City Office of Financial Empowerment.

IMPORTANT FINDINGS WITH MODEL

The following findings from this model were identified:

- The financial empowerment training must be participatory and include multiple ways to learn key information. Within the SKCABC training, two approaches stood out in particular: a) the participation of credit counseling agencies in a world café style rotation providing all case managers with the opportunity to meet with each agency and b) inclusion of resource and referral organizations in the training as both participants and presenters.

- There are opportunities for case managers and other nonprofit staff to continue their personal development by joining the Financial Education Partners Network. This group meets monthly and provides new content, as well as the opportunities to learn from other network members. The Network is one way for case managers to stay connected to ongoing financial empowerment work.

- There are opportunities to learn more about the "culture of money." In 2012 SKCABC held a panel discussion on different cultural mores and values around money and financial issues. The attendance far exceeded the organization's expectations, and they plan to provide additional opportunities to explore this topic further.

- The learn, earn, save/invest and protect framework used for the training is easy to remember and provides a natural continuum for organizing services for individual clients as well as for referral partners within a community.

- The training addresses income as well as other financial topics including credit and debt. SKCABC identified income—not having it or not having enough income to make ends meet—as the primary issue for most people.

SKCABC only conducts training evaluations with a retrospective pre-test following the training. They have not yet tracked whether case managers are actually using the information and tools provided in the training.

The Money Talks Initiative Louisville Metro / Living Cities

SITE OVERVIEW

Working through nineteen social services providers, Louisville Metro is implementing an array of financial empowerment activities that lead to financial stability with individuals and families who are currently homeless. These activities include training on banking, credit, and debt. *The Money Talks Initiative* works with case workers from partner agencies, as well as other municipal and nonprofit leaders to develop a city-wide financial empowerment framework with implementation strategies and measures. The goal is to create an operational shift from continuously providing basic needs services to increasing long-term financial and housing stability. *The Money Talks Initiative* is funded by an eighteen-month grant from Living Cities and is housed under the Louisville Metro's Department of Community Services and Revitalization (CSR).

FINANCIAL EMPOWERMENT WORK

Beginning in January, 2012, 23 social services agencies that provide homeless and housing services funded by the Community Development Block Grant (CDBG), the Emergency Services Grant (ESG) and other public and private sources were targeted to participate in the *Money Talks Initiative*. Case workers that work directly with individuals and families who are homeless receive training on personal finance topics to increase their financial knowledge. After the training, case workers are expected to use the knowledge and tools provided in the training with their clients, and to report data on specific measures to their agency management.

The Louisville affiliate of Apprisen, a nonprofit consumer credit counseling agency, conducts the training using *Money in Motion*[23], which is delivered through five separate two-hour sessions. The sessions include:

- Money Management Basics

- Budgeting Basics

- Credit Basics

- Checking and Savings Accounts

- Avoiding Identity Theft

The training includes worksheets for caseworkers to use with their clients. These worksheets include:

- How to Save Money

- Personalized Cash Flows

- Periodic Expenses

- The Cost of Living: Monthly Income and Expenses

In addition to the financial empowerment training provided to case managers, Louisville Metro is working to create a system-level financial empowerment framework that connects financial and housing stability. Using common language and common protocols, they are hoping to create city-wide impact moving people from homelessness to being housed and financially stable.

---

[23] A financial education curriculum developed by the American Center for Credit Education.

IMPORTANT FINDINGS WITH MODEL

Through interviews with case managers from two different homeless service providers trained through the *Money Talks Initiative* and involved in creating the systems-level financial empowerment framework, we learned that the training had helped them work on budgeting with their clients. Both interviewees, however, expressed an initial lack of confidence in working on other financial issues with clients when their own finances were "such a mess." However, they stressed that as they kept applying what they learned from the training, they felt their confidence increase.

Case workers also reported that they:

- Use some of the worksheets provided in the training, such as the *Cost of Living: Income and Expenses* worksheet.

- Want more training on human behaviors in relation to money to understand the reasoning behind some of the financial actions of clients. They want to understand why some clients spend money on "things that aren't basic needs."

- Find that credit and debt, budgeting, and banking are the highest priority areas for their clients.

- Refer clients to credit counselors for more intensive credit counseling.

- Agree that case workers need financial education training before they work with clients.

- Have good referrals for credit counseling and public benefits, but not for free tax preparation assistance.

- Like being in a cohort with other case workers, who meet regularly, to strengthen their own direct work with clients.

State of Minnesota

SITE OVERVIEW

Since 2004, a statewide financial literacy initiative has trained more than 1,400 case managers and other frontline staff using a financial literacy curriculum entitled *Four Cornerstones of Financial Literacy*.

In January 2012, the Minnesota Financial Literacy Interagency Work Group was formed to bring together ten state agencies that have existing programs, outreach efforts, or policy interests in financial literacy. The Work Group includes commissioners from the Departments of Commerce, Corrections, Education, Employment and Economic Development, Housing Finance, Human Rights, Military Affairs, Human Services, Revenue, and the Office of Higher Education.

The Interagency Work Group strives to achieve two goals:

- Increase communication and collaboration across the administration in order to improve and expand existing financial literacy programs, and

- Identify new ways an administration-wide partnership may help ensure Minnesotans from kindergarten to retirement have the skills, knowledge, and resources they need to achieve financial security.

To achieve these goals, the Interagency Work Group has plans to create a clearinghouse for financial literacy information, programs, and curricula; improve outreach to underserved populations such a senior citizens and youth; and encourage participation of both state employees and financial institutions in financial literacy work.

FINANCIAL EMPOWERMENT WORK

Four Cornerstones of Financial Literacy was originally developed to help Minnesota IDA programs provide financial literacy to their participants. The curriculum's four "corners" (and sessions) are:

- Budgeting to Create Savings

- Debt Reduction and Asset Building

- Building a Good Credit Rating

- Consumer Protection and Financial Institutions

This curriculum has been taught all over Minnesota in both urban and rural communities, with Native American communities and to people who speak Spanish, Hmong, and Somali, in addition to English. The curriculum is available at www.helpmnsave.com in all of the above languages so case managers and others can access the materials at any time. The website includes an "Ask a Financial Counselor" function through which questions are answered by extension educators from the University of Minnesota.

IMPORTANT FINDINGS WITH MODEL

Through interviews with case managers from Head Start, transitional housing, and car loan programs throughout Minnesota including the small cities of St. Cloud, Fergus Falls, and Marshall, we learned the following:

- A strength of *Four Cornerstones of Financial Literacy* is that it builds upon trusted advisor relationships by training case managers and other frontline staff. This makes the model distinct from approaches that rely on outside financial experts who may have little experience with the realities of low-income people and may struggle to customize information and training techniques for this population.

- While the curriculum has been delivered widely within the state and is highly regarded by many who complete the training, the State of Minnesota has not studied how the training is being used by case managers.

- Head Start Programs use the "Child Plus" data tool. All activities are documented in case notes, but there is no mechanism for culling the financial literacy work done with individuals and families from these notes. One Head Start Program conducts a follow-up interview after three months to see if parents who have received some financial literacy services are using high-cost financial services/products.

- Staff have learned different ways to "initiate the financial discussion," including using a *life satisfaction wheel* exercise and reviewing with clients the financial information that they supplied on their intake forms.

- There is high turnover among case managers and other frontline staff, which means that there is an ongoing need for additional training sessions. Access to ongoing resources is critical to the ability to continue to deliver them.

Effective practice criteria

The following criteria were identified to establish whether a given program feature should be considered an effective practice for potential adaptation for the financial empowerment training and toolkit:

- Case managers are provided with useful information they can immediately use with clients.

- Case managers receive training in ways that are engaging and reflective of the principles of adult learning.

- Case managers are provided direct training on ways to use information with clients.

- The training specifically and explicitly addresses case managers' confidence in bringing up the "financial discussion" with clients.

- In the training, case managers are provided with tools (fact sheets, work sheets, online worksheets, games, props, and links) to support their work with clients.

- Case manager confidence in using the financial information and tools and passing it on to others (their clients) is specifically addressed in the training.

- Case managers are trained to make appropriate referrals or are provided with access to a referral resource such as a person with greater expertise, handouts, or online tools and databases.

- Case managers have the opportunities to provide feedback on the training.

- Case managers are given a pre- and post-training assessment.

- Case managers have a simple system to track the time and content they are passing on to clients.

- Financial educators or case managers can track outcomes related to financial empowerment that is integrated into case management services.

- Where the information is not being shared with clients, case managers (or the financial education providers) understand through interviews, focus groups or some other empirical method the reasons case managers are not using the information with clients.

- Case managers are enrolling in training because their executives or supervisors have directed them or expect them to do so.

- Executives or supervisors have incorporated financial education performance objectives as part of the review process for case managers.

- The model used is flexible (meaning it can be adapted for different situations, target populations or communities).

- The model used is replicable in less resource-intensive environments such as smaller or rural communities.

APPENDIX C:

Case manager and financial education provider outcomes

Outcomes are changes or benefits to the target audience as a result of the strategies/activities.

Case manager outcomes

SHORT-TERM

Case managers may experience:

Increased awareness of the ways in which the outcomes of financial empowerment training align with their own program outcomes.

Increased confidence in their own knowledge about core financial management topics:
- Getting and managing income
- Using a budget or managing cash flow
- Managing debt and debt collections
- Improving credit reports and scores
- Paying bills on time
- For those who qualify, using public benefits and other resources to improve cash flow
- Saving for emergencies and long term goals
- Filing for tax credits and using tax refunds to eliminate debt, save and build assets
- Using appropriate financial institutions, products and services to manage income and expenses
- Building assets beyond savings
- Knowing some basic consumer protection laws and the agency framework designed to protect individuals from concentrated powers of business and financial services

Increased ability to provide the right financial information at the right time in the context of their case work with clients.

Increased ability to use specific tools to help clients reach their own goals in different cultural and situational contexts.

Increased ability to understand the reasons people make financial decisions from a values, beliefs, and attitudes perspective as well as from a behavioral economics perspective.

Increased ability to make appropriate and specific referrals to help clients manage their financial challenges.

INTERMEDIATE

As a result of their work with case managers, <u>clients</u> may know:

- One new strategy for reducing or eliminating debt
- The process for conducting debt validation and verification
- One new system for keeping track of bills and paying bills on time
- One new way to project cash flow and anticipate where they may be short on cash or other resources as well as strategies for managing cash shortfalls
- The reason to explore whether they are eligible for benefits
- At least one website or agency where they can be screened for benefits
- The reason for saving $500 to $1,000 in an emergency savings account
- At least one bank and one nonbank option for the emergency savings fund that is safe and secure
- At least one strategy for automating saving or regularly finding money to save
- One resource for getting taxes prepared for free
- At least one reason for planning the use of the tax refund
- Identify financial products that will help them improve their money management efficiency and decrease their costs
- Where to get more help for debt management, credit building, budgeting, paying bills, and using financial products and services
- How to access resources on the CFPB website
- How to submit a complaint to the CFPB
- Increased confidence in managing finances

LONG-TERM

- Improvements in economic conditions (<u>both case managers and clients</u>):
- Increase in income
- Decrease in debt-to- income ratio
- Decrease in expense-to- income ratio
- Increase in credit scores
- Decrease in income spent on late fees or other fines related to late bill payments
- There is a potential for decrease in use of agency services
- Decrease in use of debt to close monthly income gap (income and expenses balance from week to week)
- $500 to $1,000 in emergency savings
- Increase in use of community resources to help with financial issues (as a result of appropriate and specific referrals)
- Decrease in stress resulting from financial instability (<u>their own and for their clients</u>)
- Increase in goal attainment (<u>their own and for their clients</u>)
- As financial stability increases there is a potential for decrease in clients' use of agency services.

Financial education provider outcomes

IMMEDIATE

Increased understanding of the barriers and challenges case managers face in providing financial education to clients as well as the opportunities.

Increased understanding of the context in which case managers provide financial education.

Increased ability to provide relevant and specific training to case managers that:

- Improves their confidence in talking about financial issues with clients.
- Increases their basic financial knowledge.
- Increases their ability to use specific tools with clients and within different cultural and situational contexts.
- Increases their ability to provide the right financial content at the right time with clients.
- Increases their ability to make appropriate and specific referrals, and
- Increases their ability to use the resources of the CFPB.

INTERMEDIATE

Case managers receiving the training will have:

Increased confidence in their own knowledge about core financial management topics:

- Managing debt and debt collections
- Improving credit reports and scores
- Paying bills on time
- Managing cash flow
- Using public benefits and other resources to improve cash flow
- Saving for emergencies and long term goals
- Using tax refunds to eliminate debt, to save and to build assets
- Using appropriate financial products and services to manage income and expenses

Increased ability to identify financial education teachable moments in the context of their case work with clients.

Increased ability to make appropriate and specific referrals to help clients manage their financial challenges.

APPENDIX D:

Additional programs interviewed for scan

Cities for Financial Empowerment (National) is a multi-city initiative that brings together pioneering municipal governments from across the country that have begun to use their power and positions to advance innovative financial empowerment initiatives.

Four Bands Community Fund (Eagle Butte, S.D.) serves tribal members and provides training for community-based organization staff and helps community partners integrate financial education into the services they provide.

Headstart Pilot Project (Massachusetts) pioneered a cross-generational approach to financial education by introducing children to fundamental and age-appropriate financial concepts in the classroom, while their parents participated in financial education sessions in the morning or early evening.

Headstart Pilot Project (State of Pennsylvania) targets financial empowerment training to teachers, home visitors and family service coordinators who work with parents to develop Family Service Development Plans.

Hopelink (Bellevue, Wash.) is a community action program which uses case management to help clients reach self-sufficiency and uses an in-house curriculum that was developed to help case managers talk about money with clients.

LISC Financial Opportunity Centers are located in 23 cities and provide career and personal financial service centers focused on the financial bottom line for low- to-moderate income individuals.

Rise Foundation (Memphis, Tenn.) provides training to employees of United Way-funded organizations using its own curriculum—*Common Cents*—within the workplace. They bring the training to the nonprofit organizations to make attendance easy for the nonprofit, frontline staff, and case managers.

United Way of Greater Chattanooga (Chattanooga, Tenn.) provides financial education and other financial empowerment services to urban and rural families by training staff of faith-based organizations, nonprofits, and other partners who directly serve families in need of assistance.

United Way of King County (Seattle, Wash.) provides financial empowerment training to Employment Cohort agency staff so they can integrate financial education into the employment services offered to their clients.

United Way of Silicon Valley (San Jose, Calif.) works with partner organizations on setting up a credit coaching programs that are staffed by both paid staff and volunteers and conducts delivery of their Credit Coaching Training for paid staff and volunteers who want to become credit coaches.